My First
Travel Book

This book belongs to:

....

From: Captain Herbie

& Ane Oluts

....

Date:

11/21/15

....

Signed by:

Oluts

....

My First Travel Books

The Seven Wonders of The World

with Captain Frankie

Anna Othitis

My First Travel Books

The Seven Wonders of the World

© Anna Othitis 2014

ISBN: 978-1-910115-18-3

ALL RIGHTS RESERVED.

Cover design and image editing by Cecelia Morgan

Editing and Formatting by LionheART Publishing House, part of LionheART Galleries Ltd

My special thanks to my son the pilot
Frankie Othitis, "Captain Frankie"
who is a pilot in real life, for his inspiration and
encouragement to continue to author another
children's book, a series of
"My First Travel Book" with more adventurous
travels on our amazing "Angelic Airlines",
discovering and learning about the wonderful world
that we live in.

To my husband George and sons Johnny and Elia
for their wonderful encouragement, inspiration,
praise and support at all times. You are all such
shining stars of love and affection in my life.

Of course to my wonderful little—and some big—
readers for their support.

Thank You so Much

"Welcome aboard Angelic Airlines. This is your Captain Frankie, and I will be flying you to yet more very popular destinations and places around the world. This time we will be visiting the

'Seven Wonders Of The World'

Please fasten your seat belts, stow your bags, make yourselves comfortable and get ready for a smooth take off on another wondrous journey into the deep blue skies."

The Beautiful Colorful Country Flags
of the Seven Wonders of Our World

Mexico

Brazil

Peru

Jordan

Italy

India

China

Welcome to Angelic Airlines with your pilot Captain Frankie. I will be taking you to see our beautiful "Seven Natural Wonders Of The World".

Fasten your seat belts, stow your luggage, relax and enjoy another wonderful adventure flying with us.

This is a map of our world which shows you where you can find our Seven Wonders of the World. What a big world we live in so wide and spread apart and over the oceans

The "New" Seven Wonders of the World
Announced On July 7, 2007

Chichen Itza, Mexico - Mayan City

Christ the Redeemer, Brazil - Large Statue

The Great Wall of China

Machu Picchu, Peru

Petra, Jordan - Ancient City

The Roman Colosseum, Italy

The Taj Mahal, India

Welcome aboard once again lovely young
"World Globe Trotters"
our amazing little passengers.

So very wonderful and happy to see you join
us once again on our Angelic Airlines with our
safe and friendly pilot, your Captain Frankie.

He is excited to take you on another flight around the world to learn and visit more interesting and famous sites in our world.

Now remember on out last travel trip we discovered and saw the "Seven Wonders of our Earth", this time we are visiting the "Seven Wonders of our WORLD".

Isn't so special that we have so many wonders to visit and see?

Stow your bags overhead, take your seats, and fasten your seat belts for our take off on a smooth flight together through the clouds. It is a lovely sunny day today and I hope you enjoy your flight. Make yourselves comfortable, we have lots of healthy drinks and meals for you.

Chichen Itza

Castillo – Mexico

Our first visit on this trip will be to visit Tinum, Mexico to tour a pyramid in Mexico built by the Mayans many years ago in 600 AD. It is named Chichen Itza, which means "at the mouth of the well of the Itza".

Look at that ancient city where the patient Mayans built their pyramid stone by stone, just like a square ice cream cone, with stairs so steep and deep for the ancient people to climb up to meet and sleep, have a feast and have the chance to dance to the merry music.

The four sides of the pyramid have stairways and fairways with carved heads of a serpent. It is one of the oldest buildings in Mexico and is visited by many tourists who go to see the light-and-shadow effect on the Temple of Kukulkan, which looks like the feathered serpent god.

You can crawl down the side of the pyramid and go inside the many chambers to see the old pottery and stone-carved art.

When standing on the steps, if you clap your hands you can hear echoes because it is hollow and the sound bounces off the walls.

In what country is this?

Who built the pyramid?

How do you get to the top?

What is inside the pyramid?

Christ The Redeemer Statue

– Rio de Janeiro, Brazil

Take a look below as we fly over this massive mountain with a statue built on it.

Christ The Redeemer stands on a pedestal, the statue is one hundred and twenty feet tall on top of the Corcovado Mountain of the Tijuca Forest National Park with wide-open arms stretched and holding out its palms.

It wears its long hair so lovely and fair with a long pleated gown looking down over the largest natural harbor and the city of Rio de Janeiro. What a beautiful sight to see! Now be careful, children, this is very high up—it's dangerous and very windy up there. Look at those birds, how high they fly.

The breathtaking statue weighs six hundred and thirty five tons—it's as heavy as a crane.

In Brazil, the famous statue is a symbol of Christianity and stands high up on the top of Mt. Corcovado. This mountain is two thousand three hundred feet high and visitors like to see the huge wide bay with a bird's eye view. The statue was build out of reinforced concrete instead of steel.

People drive up under the statue and the Catholic people hold baptisms and weddings here.

How tall is the statue?

What does this statue wear?

What is the name of the mountain on which the statue stands?

How much does the statue weigh?

Machu Picchu – Peru

I hope you enjoyed your journey to the highest point in Brazil and now we are taking off to go and see a beautiful dry stone wall temple of the Inca Empire.

The Machu Picchu, in Peru—look at this Temple of the Sun. Oh what fun! And look—the Room of the Three Windows, which the ancient people built on a mountain ridge above the sacred valley. The emperor, their king, would have his people sing and their voices would ring into the valley.

It was also named the "Lost City of the Incas" where they studied the stars in the sky.

Far away below is the Urubamba River, and see those cliffs? They look like huge slipping slides where we can slide and ride down to the river and go and splash about below. Captain Frankie, can we go and play for the day?

The mist rises from the river like figurines and shadows like Halloween hallows. Spring water runs from the mountain, trickling down, far below, watering the trees and grass.

The city was a military secret, and its deep, steep mountains were a hiding place for the Incas to see the enemies below. Imagine there were two hundred buildings on the mountaintop—their stones and mud was carried and pulled by men up these steep mountains.

This city was hidden for a long time and eventually found in these very high, steep mountains where people now go up by buses to see the Lost City of the Incas.

In what country is this temple?

Who lived in this hidden city?

What was it also named?

Where does the mist rise from?

The Ancient City of Petra – Jordan

Well, children, did you enjoy your visit to the lost city of the ancient people of Inca? That was fun to see how they lived hidden away all these years. There is so much still to be discovered on this Earth from so many thousands of years ago.

Are you enjoying yourselves, learning about the ancient times and how the people lived in those days? It's very interesting to see how we live now with all our comforts.

Now we are about to see another old building in Jordan. Look at the Dead Sea and how it runs into the Gulf of Aqaba where the Nabataean Empire carved the building Petra out of large cliffs and controlled all of Israel, Egypt, Syria and Saudi Arabia in the Middle East.

Look at the rose-red city, it looks like a city built with Lego the color of the desert sands. We can walk the path through the dark, narrow gorge, but we might need a torch, and let us make sure we do not scorch in the strong sun. Wear your climbing boots and watch those tree roots and grass. Look at those strong pillars—they look such thrillers holding up the tombs and all those rooms.

This city was given as a gift to Obodas the God. The Nabataeans worshipped the Arab gods and goddesses and many beautiful statues are carved in the rock showing these deities.

Where do we find this old city?

What sea is close by Jordan?

Who was the city given to as a gift?

Who did they worship?

Colosseum in Rome – Italy

Walking and climbing was fun but hard work. We are ready for take off now, the airplane engines are running and ready to roar back into the skies over the desert. Off to Europe we go, it's time to visit the 'Big Boot' of Europe—Rome, Italy.

"Buongiorno, bella mattina" Good morning, what a beautiful morning.

Do you see the Colosseum in Rome? Round and huge just like a baseball field surrounded by a thick wall so tall with huge arched windows and a breeze—mind you do not sneeze.

The Colosseum was once used for contests where slaves would fight one another as sport to amuse the people of the ancient Roman Empire.

Fifty thousand people could be seated in this huge arena to watch the shows. There were special boxes for the Emperor and his family to sit, and around that was seating made of stone and marble where the guests would sit on cushions.

The arena was two hundred and seventy two feet with a wooden floor covered by sand. Underneath were separate tunnels where different animals would be kept to perform like a circus.

Today the Colosseum is used for Roman Catholic ceremonies.

So, children, we can now understand how our stadiums of today came about. Is it not amazing that from so many years ago, the old is made new like our stadiums and arenas?

What does Italy look like?

What continent is Italy on?

What was the Colosseum used for?

What was the arena used for?

Taj Mahal – India

Come on aboard now as we prepare to go to India in Asia to visit and see the famous Taj Mahal built by Emperor Shah Jahan in honor of his wife.

This beautiful dome was his home, made of white marble with lovely gardens open at all hours. The pillars remind us of tiny lighthouses standing tall and in a straight line like little soldiers on guard welcoming us. Let us march down the path to the amazing Taj Mahal in single file with great style.

The marble dome that surmounts the tomb is the most spectacular feature with its height of about one hundred and fifty feet. The dome is often called an 'onion dome' and is decorated with traditional Hindu symbols. The decoration and fine art work is what a lot of tourists come to see. The inside walls are all finely decorated with such fine and detailed carved artwork, like strips of beautiful lace.

Paradise gardens hold beautiful fruit trees, roses and daffodils of all colors and scents. Four rivers flow from a spring mountain, which separates this floral garden into north, west, south and east. What a true peaceful experience of paradise in our world, so calm and quiet with sweet floral scents, a true sign of love that the emperor had for his wife.

The wonderful Taj Mahal standing so bright, tall and perfectly proud.

In which country is the Taj Mahal?

Who was it built for?

What is the dome often called?

How many rivers flow from the mountain?

Great Wall of China

This is our final destination and the most wonderful of the Seven Wonders Of Our World with your pilot Captain Frankie. I trust you have enjoyed this wonderful educational and inspirational flight.

To the Great Wall of China we go. Look down below at this great long wall which will never fall, stretching from east to west it is but the best. We will have to take a rest walking along this strong stone wall.

We have to balance ourselves as we do on a tight rope when we go down the slopes of the hills over the rivers and streams twisting and winding like an earth dragon.

The Great Wall of China is a marvelous wonder built with stones and earth going through and over mountain ranges.

This great wall was used to protect the Chinese Empire from attacks from the north. It stretches over four thousand miles in the north part of China and is thirty feet wide, it was built by millions of Chinese people.

The main Great Wall line stretches from Shanhaiguan in the east, to Lope Lake in the west. All the walls put together measure thirteen thousand one hundred and seventy one miles.

Imagine how long it would take us to walk all of the wall!

In which country do we find this Great Wall?

What was the wall built with?

What was the Great Wall built for?

What was the Great Wall of China built?

Captain Frankie's Quiz Questions

Children, do you know which are the

Seven Wonders of the World?

Speak them out loud with me:

Chichen Itza

Christ the Redeemer Statue

Machu Picchu

The Ancient City of Petra

The Colosseum

Taj Mahal

The Great Wall of China

Girls and boys, this once again brings us to the end of our wonderful journey traveling to our Seven Wonders of the World. I hope that you had a fun and pleasant flight. I thank you for flying with me on Angelic Airlines. We got to see and learn about more wonderful wonders of our world.

Let us look after our world and its environment to preserve these wonders.
We will be back soon with more
Angelic Airline Adventures

Stay on board with your Captain Frankie.
I hope to see you all again very soon and I always welcome you aboard.

"We Are The World, We Are The People Living In It"

Children, here is your boarding pass and airplane ticket for Our Next World Travel

SEE YOU SOON AND REMEMBER, TAKE CARE OF OUR EARTH

More Angelic Airline Adventures coming soon, with your friendly Captain Frankie.

25591215R00018

Made in the USA
Middletown, DE
03 November 2015